Bible Approved Holidays

Ending Pagan Rituals

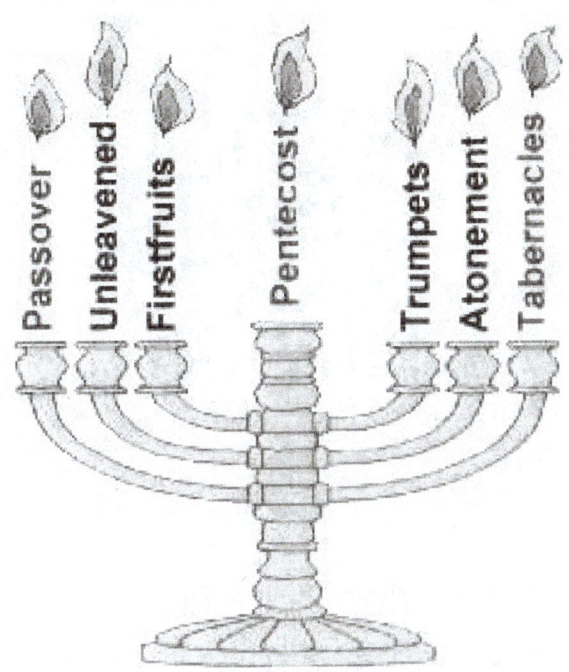

By Karajah Yashar

BLACKSTONE PUBLISHING

Orlando, FL 2024

Bible Approved Holidays: Ending Pagan Rituals

ISBN: 978-1-962691-27-7

First Edition: May 2024

This book is dedicated to my cherished friends and beloved family members, whose love and companionship enrich my life in countless ways. Though I cannot partake in certain rituals that do not align with my faith, my love for you remains unwavering. Additionally, this dedication is extended to all those who are passionately dedicated to their faith, fervently seeking wisdom, and tirelessly striving to deepen their connection with the Lord. May we continue to journey together, sharing in the pursuit of spiritual growth and enlightenment.

"And this day shall be unto you for a memorial; and ye shall keep it a feast to the LORD throughout your generations; ye shall keep it a feast by an ordinance for ever."

Exodus 12:14

Table of Contents

Why Celebrate Biblical Holidays?

In the tapestry of biblical tradition, holidays stand as pillars of remembrance, celebration, and spiritual renewal. These sacred occasions, spanning from ancient times to the present day, hold profound significance for believers worldwide. Understanding the holidays of the Bible and their importance in fostering holiness illuminates the essence of faith and community. Celebrating the holidays of the Bible fosters a deep sense of connection to the sacred narrative of salvation history. These rituals serve as windows into the divine, inviting believers to encounter God's presence in their midst. Moreover, these holidays reinforce communal bonds, uniting believers across generations and cultures in a shared journey of faith.

The Bible unequivocally condemns the worship of false gods and the participation in pagan rituals. In Exodus 20:3-5, God commands, "You shall have no other gods before me. You shall not make for yourself an image in the form of anything in heaven above or on the earth beneath or in the waters below. You shall not bow down to them or worship them." This commandment underscores the exclusivity of worship owed to God and prohibits the veneration of idols or false deities.

Despite these biblical admonitions, many traditional Christian holidays, including Easter and Christmas, have been influenced by pagan customs and practices. Easter, for example, has pagan origins stemming from ancient spring festivals celebrating fertility and the renewal of life. The name "Easter" itself is derived from Eostre, a pagan goddess of spring and fertility worshipped by Germanic peoples. Elements of Easter, such as the Easter bunny and colored eggs, have pagan roots and symbolize fertility and rebirth.

Similarly, the celebration of Christmas has pagan elements intertwined with Christian traditions. The date of December 25 was chosen by early

Christians to coincide with the winter solstice and the Roman festival of Saturnalia, a time of feasting and revelry. Many customs associated with Christmas, such as decorating evergreen trees, exchanging gifts, and singing carols, have pagan origins and were incorporated into Christian observances over time.

The association of Easter and Christmas with pagan customs raises important questions for believers about the authenticity of these holidays and their compatibility with biblical teachings. While some argue that the Christianization of pagan festivals was a deliberate effort to Christianize cultural practices and bring pagans into the fold of Christianity, it must be viewed with caution, mindful of the biblical warnings against syncretism and idolatry. In Jeremiah 10:2 God specifically tells us not to deal in pagan ways. "Thus saith the LORD, Learn not the way of the heathen, and be not dismayed at the signs of heaven; for the heathen are dismayed at them."

Believers should prioritize celebrating the high holy days of the Bible over pagan celebrations because these biblical festivals are rooted in God's commands and reflect His redemptive plan for humanity. Unlike pagan holidays, which often promote values and practices contrary to biblical teachings, the high holy days, such as Passover, Pentecost, and the Feast of Tabernacles, serve as reminders of God's faithfulness, deliverance, and provision. By observing these sacred festivals, believers not only honor God's commands but also deepen their understanding of His character and purposes. Additionally, celebrating the high holy days fosters spiritual growth, community fellowship, and a deeper connection to God's covenant promises, enriching believers' faith journey and nurturing a lifestyle of holiness and obedience.

The High Holy days and Feast Days

The major Biblical Holidays are called High Holy Days, biblical feasts, or appointed times. There are also Minor Feast Day celebrations. There are a total of Seven High Holy Days given in the Bible. They hold profound significance in Hebrew tradition and hold spiritual relevance for all followers of Jesus Christ. These sacred observances, outlined in the Old Testament, mark key moments in the relationship between God and His people, serving as reminders of His faithfulness, provision, and redemptive plan for humanity. Understanding the significance of these feasts illuminates the tapestry of biblical history and invites believers to engage with the timeless truths embedded within them.

The Seven High Holy days of the Bible:

1. **Passover (Pesach):** Passover, the first of the high holy days, commemorates the Exodus narrative, where God liberated the Israelites from slavery in Egypt. In the New Testament,

Passover is the time of the sacrificial death of Jesus Christ, who became the ultimate Passover Lamb, offering redemption and freedom from the bondage of sin.

2. **Unleavened Bread (Chag HaMatzot):** Immediately following Passover is the Feast of Unleavened Bread, during which leavened bread is removed from homes and only unleavened bread is consumed for seven days. This feast symbolizes the haste with which the Israelites left Egypt and serves as a reminder of the importance of spiritual purity and obedience.

3. **Firstfruits (Yom HaBikkurim):** The Feast of Firstfruits occurs during the Passover season and marks the offering of the first fruits of the barley harvest to God. It symbolizes gratitude for God's provision and acknowledges His sovereignty over the harvest. For Christians, Firstfruits holds significance as Jesus' resurrection occurred

during this time, signifying the first fruits of a new spiritual harvest.

4. **Pentecost (Shavuot):** Fifty days after the Feast of Firstfruits, Pentecost is celebrated, commemorating the giving of the Torah at Mount Sinai. It is a time of rejoicing and thanksgiving for the Law, which serves as a guide for righteous living. In the Christian tradition, Pentecost also marks the outpouring of the Holy Spirit upon the disciples, empowering them for ministry and inaugurating the age of the Church.

5. **Trumpets (Rosh HaShanah):** Rosh HaShanah, or the Feast of Trumpets, heralds the beginning of the sacred seventh month and is characterized by the blowing of the shofar (ram's horn). It is a time of reflection, repentance, and renewal, as believers prepare for the upcoming Day of Atonement.

6. **Day of Atonement (Yom Kippur):** The most solemn of the high holy days, Yom Kippur is

a day of fasting, prayer, and repentance, during which sins are confessed and atoned for. It symbolizes reconciliation with God and one another, emphasizing the importance of humility and forgiveness in the pursuit of holiness.

7. **Tabernacles (Sukkot):** The Feast of Tabernacles is a week-long celebration of God's provision during the wilderness wanderings, marked by the construction of temporary shelters called sukkot. It is a time of joy, fellowship, and gratitude for God's presence and protection. In Christian theology, Tabernacles foreshadows the ultimate fulfillment of God's kingdom, when He will dwell among His people in perfect unity and peace.

The Seven High Holy Days of the Bible are not merely historical commemorations but profound expressions of faith, identity, and covenantal relationship with God. Through these sacred observances, believers are invited to remember God's faithfulness, to recommit themselves to His commandments, and to anticipate the fulfillment of His redemptive plan. As Christians, we recognize the spiritual significance of these feasts and find deeper meaning in the life, death, and resurrection of Jesus Christ, who fulfills and embodies the ultimate meaning of these holy days.

Ceremonial Observances:

Sabbaths: The Sabbath, a sacred day of rest and worship, holds profound significance in the Bible. It is rooted in the creation narrative of Genesis, where God rested on the seventh day after creating the world. The Sabbath serves as a weekly reminder of God's sovereignty, provision, and invitation to enter into His rest. The Sabbath is mandated in the Ten Commandments as well.

New Moons: In the Bible, New Moons are considered a time of ceremonial observance, where people gather for worship and community activities. New Moons mark the beginning of each lunar month and hold symbolic significance as a time of spiritual renewal and reflection, echoing themes of God's faithfulness and the cyclical nature of time within the context of creation and redemption.

Minor Festivals:

Purim: Purim is a Hebrew holiday commemorating the deliverance of the Israelite people from a plot to exterminate them, as recorded in the Book of Esther. It is celebrated with feasting, reading the Book of Esther, giving to the poor, and exchanging gifts.

Hanukkah (Chanukah): Hanukkah, also known as the Festival of Lights, celebrates the rededication of the Second Temple in Jerusalem after its desecration by the forces of Antiochus IV Epiphanes. It is observed with the lighting of the Hanukkah menorah, feasting, and playing games.

Passover

Passover, or Pesach in Hebrew, stands as one of the most significant and sacred holidays for the Hebrew people. Its origins trace back to the Exodus narrative, a defining moment in Hebrew history when God liberated the Israelites from slavery in Egypt. Passover commemorates this pivotal event, serving as a powerful symbol of divine deliverance, redemption, and covenantal faithfulness.

For Hebrews, Passover is more than just a historical remembrance; it is a deeply spiritual and communal experience that connects them to their identity as God's chosen people. The observance of Passover is rooted in the commandments given to Moses in the book of Exodus, where God instructs the Israelites to commemorate the event annually as a perpetual ordinance.

Passover is celebrated with a ceremonial meal which takes place on the first night of the holiday. Central to the Passover meal is the retelling of the

Exodus narrative, emphasizing the themes of slavery, liberation, and redemption. Participants engage in symbolic acts such as the consumption of unleavened bread (matzah) to represent the haste with which the Israelites left Egypt, the eating of bitter herbs to recall the bitterness of slavery, and the partaking of a roasted lamb shank bone as a reminder of the sacrificial lamb whose blood spared the Israelites from the Angel of Death.

In the New Testament, Jesus Christ is the ultimate Passover Lamb, whose sacrificial death and resurrection fulfill the typology of the Passover lamb in the Old Testament. Just as the blood of the Passover lamb protected the Israelites from death, so too does the blood of Jesus provide salvation and deliverance from sin and spiritual death.

Believers are called to commemorate and celebrate Passover as a perpetual memorial, as instructed in the Bible. In Exodus 12:14, God commands the Israelites, "This day shall be for you a memorial day, and you shall keep it as a feast to the Lord; throughout your generations, as a statute forever, you shall keep it as a feast."

Therefore, believers have a profound spiritual heritage in the observance of Passover. It serves as a powerful reminder of God's faithfulness, His redemptive power, and His enduring covenant with His people. As such, celebrating Passover allows believers to reaffirm their faith, strengthen their communal bonds, and deepen their connection to the timeless truths embedded within this sacred holiday.

How to Celebrate:

For anyone celebrating the Passover, approaching the High Holy Day with reverence, humility, and a desire to learn can enrich their faith journey and deepen their understanding of God's redemptive plan. Here are some practical steps for Believers to celebrate the day:

Learn about the significance of Passover: Take the time to study the biblical narrative of the Exodus and the instructions for Passover found in the book of Exodus, particularly chapters 12-13. Understanding the historical and theological significance of Passover will provide context for its observance. Several verses in the New Testament reference Passover, highlighting its significance in the life and teachings of Jesus Christ and its connection to the fulfillment of Old Testament prophecy. Here are some key New Testament verses about Passover:

- *Matthew 26:17-19*: "Now the first day of the feast of unleavened bread the disciples came to Jesus, saying unto him, Where wilt thou that we prepare for thee to eat the passover? And he said, Go into the city to such a man, and say unto him, The Master saith, My time is at hand; I will keep the passover at thy house with my disciples. And the disciples did as Jesus had appointed them; and they made ready the passover."

- *Mark 14:12-16*: "And the first day of unleavened bread, when they killed the passover, his disciples said unto him, Where wilt thou that we go and prepare that thou mayest eat the passover? And he sendeth forth two of his disciples, and saith unto them, Go ye into the city, and there shall meet you a man bearing a pitcher of water: follow him. And wheresoever he shall go in, say ye to the goodman of the house, The Master saith, Where is the guestchamber, where I shall eat the passover with my disciples? And he will shew you a large upper room furnished and prepared: there make ready for us. And his disciples went forth, and came into the city, and found as he had said unto them: and they made ready the passover."

- *Luke 22:7-13*: "Then came the day of unleavened bread, when the passover must be killed. And he sent Peter and John, saying, Go and prepare us the passover, that we may eat. And they said unto him, Where wilt thou that we prepare? And he said unto them, Behold, when ye are entered into the city, there shall a man meet you, bearing a pitcher of water; follow him into the house where he entereth in. And ye shall say unto the goodman of the house, The Master saith unto thee, Where is the guestchamber, where I shall eat the passover with my disciples? And he shall shew you a large upper room furnished: there make ready. And they went, and found as he had said unto them: and they made ready the passover."
- *John 13:1-2*: "Now before the feast of the passover, when Jesus knew that his

hour was come that he should depart out of this world unto the Father, having loved his own which were in the world, he loved them unto the end. And supper being ended, the devil having now put into the heart of Judas Iscariot, Simon's son, to betray him."

These verses depict the preparations for and the observance of the Passover meal, often referred to as the Last Supper, by Jesus and his disciples. They highlight the significance of Passover in the life and ministry of Jesus, as well as its connection to his impending sacrifice and the establishment of the new covenant.

The Apostle Paul makes several references to Passover in his writings, highlighting its significance within the context of Christ and the New Covenant. One of the key passages where Paul discusses Passover is found in 1 Corinthians 5:7-8:

"Purge out therefore the old leaven, that ye may be a new lump, as ye are unleavened. For even Christ our passover is sacrificed for us: Therefore let us keep the feast, not with old leaven, neither with the leaven of malice and wickedness; but with the unleavened bread of sincerity and truth."

In this passage, Paul employs imagery related to the Feast of Unleavened Bread, which immediately follows Passover in Biblical tradition, to convey spiritual truths to the Corinthian believers. He emphasizes the need for spiritual purity and sincerity among followers of Christ, urging them to remove the "old leaven" of sin and corruption from their lives. Paul then makes a profound theological statement by declaring, "For even Christ our passover is sacrificed for us." Here, Paul identifies Jesus Christ as the ultimate Passover Lamb whose sacrificial death atones for the sins of humanity. This declaration underscores the central role of Jesus' death and resurrection in fulfilling the typology of the Passover lamb in the

Old Testament and inaugurating a new covenant between God and humanity.

Furthermore, Paul's exhortation to "keep the feast" carries both literal and metaphorical significance. While Paul likely encourages the Corinthians to observe the Lord's Supper, which commemorates Jesus' sacrificial death and resurrection, his language also suggests a broader call to live in alignment with the spiritual truths represented by Passover. Believers are called to embrace the values of sincerity and truth, rejecting the "leaven" of sin and embracing the transformative power of Christ's redemption.

Overall, Paul's teachings on Passover emphasize the continuity between Old Testament rituals and Christian theology, as well as the transformative impact of Jesus' death and resurrection on the lives of believers. Through his writings, Paul invites believers to participate in the spiritual realities symbolized by Passover, embracing their identity as recipients of God's grace and heirs of the new covenant established through Christ's sacrifice.

Host a Passover Dinner: Gather friends, family, or fellow believers to host a Passover Dinner in your home or church. Utilize resources such as Passover guides specifically designed for Christ believers. Incorporate elements of faith such as prayers, hymns, and reflections on the significance of Jesus as the Passover Lamb.

Prepare a Passover meal: While it is called a feast day, the High Holy day feasts are not times for gluttony as many pagan traditions encourage. The Passover meal is very basic with only a few foods on the menu. Whether attending a feast or hosting your own, prepare traditional Passover foods such as unleavened bread (matzah), bitter herbs (such as horseradish), and a roasted lamb shank bone. These foods symbolize various aspects of the Exodus story and provide a sensory experience of the holiday. Because animal sacrifice is done away with under the New Covenant, the unleavened bread which represents the body of Christ can be utilized to replace the lamb if desired. Christ is now the Passover lamb. Red wine or Grape juice is also consumed representing the blood of Jesus. Make sure to pray over the body and the blood before consumption.

1. *Reflect on the spiritual significance*: Take time for personal reflection and meditation on the spiritual lessons of Passover. Consider the themes of liberation, redemption, and covenantal faithfulness, and how they resonate with your own journey of faith. Meditate on Jesus as the ultimate Passover Lamb and His sacrifice for the forgiveness of sins.

2. *Engage in acts of service and charity*: Passover emphasizes themes of justice, compassion, and solidarity with the oppressed. Take this opportunity to engage in acts of service and charity, reflecting God's heart for the marginalized and

downtrodden. Seek ways to advocate for justice and freedom in your community and beyond.

3. Continue the tradition: Make Passover observance an annual tradition in your Christ led walk. Each year, revisit the Exodus narrative and the gospel, deepen your understanding of Passover's significance, and celebrate with renewed gratitude for God's deliverance and redemption.

By embracing Passover with humility, reverence, and a desire to learn, believers can enrich their spiritual journey and draw closer to God's redemptive plan for humanity. As they participate in the traditions and rituals of Passover, they can deepen their appreciation for the biblical roots of their faith and the enduring significance of Jesus as the Passover Lamb.

Feast of Unleavened Bread

The Feast of Unleavened Bread is a significant holiday in Biblical tradition. It is closely associated with Passover and follows immediately after it, lasting for seven days. This feast holds deep spiritual and symbolic meaning, emphasizing themes of purity, obedience, and liberation.

In Hebrew tradition, the Feast of Unleavened Bread commemorates the haste with which the Israelites left Egypt during the Exodus. It is a reminder of their journey from slavery to freedom and the importance of spiritual purity in their relationship with God. During this time, leavened bread is avoided, and only unleavened bread, known as matzah, is consumed. The removal of leaven symbolizes the removal of sin and impurity from one's life, while the consumption of unleavened bread serves as a tangible reminder of the Israelites' dependence on God's provision and protection during their wilderness wanderings.

The celebration of the Feast of Unleavened Bread typically involves special meals, prayers, and rituals. Families gather to share symbolic foods and retell the story of the Exodus, emphasizing the themes of deliverance and gratitude. The removal of leaven from the home is a ceremonial process, often accompanied by thorough cleaning and preparation to ensure the removal of all traces of leavened products.

In the New Testament, the significance of the Feast of Unleavened Bread is affirmed and expanded upon. Jesus Christ's death and resurrection occurred during the time of Passover and the Feast of Unleavened Bread, imbuing these holidays with added significance for believers. The removal of leaven symbolizes the removal of sin, and the consumption of unleavened bread represents the purity and holiness that believers are called to embrace.

Furthermore, the Apostle Paul draws upon the symbolism of the Feast of Unleavened Bread in his teachings to the early Christian communities. In 1 Corinthians 5:7-8, Paul exhorts believers to embrace spiritual purity and sincerity, drawing parallels between the removal of leaven and the removal of sin from their lives through the sacrifice of Jesus Christ.

The Feast of Unleavened Bread holds profound significance in Hebrew and Christ centered traditions. It serves as a reminder of God's deliverance and provision, a call to spiritual purity and obedience, and a symbol of the transformative power of redemption. As believers commemorate this feast, they are invited to reflect on the timeless truths it embodies and to embrace the call to live lives marked by sincerity, truth, and devotion to God.

How to Celebrate:

Celebrating the Feast of Unleavened Bread is a significant aspect of Christ centered faith, rooted in both biblical tradition and the spiritual journey of believers. Lasting for seven days immediately following Passover, this feast holds deep symbolic meaning, emphasizing themes of purity, redemption, and devotion to God. Here's how believers can celebrate the Feast of Unleavened Bread in a manner that honors biblical principles and fosters spiritual growth:

1. *Preparation and Reflection*: Before the Feast of Unleavened Bread begins, participants can engage in a period of preparation and reflection. This involves examining their hearts and lives for any "leaven," symbolic of sin and impurity, and seeking repentance and cleansing through prayer and confession. It's a time to reflect on the significance of the feast and its relevance to their spiritual journey.

2. *Removing Leaven*: On the eve of the feast, families can engage in the ceremonial removal of leaven from their homes. This

involves a thorough cleaning and removal of all leavened products, symbolizing the removal of sin and impurity from their lives. This act serves as a tangible reminder of the call to live lives of holiness and devotion to God.

3. *Eating Unleavened Bread:* Throughout the week of the Feast of Unleavened Bread, believers can partake in eating unleavened bread, also known as matzah. This bread, made without leaven, serves as a symbol of purity and sincerity in their devotion to God. It's a reminder of the haste with which the Israelites left Egypt during the Exodus and the need for spiritual readiness in following God's lead.

4. *Scripture Reading and Study:* Participants can dedicate time each day during the Feast of Unleavened Bread to reading and studying Scripture, particularly passages related to the Exodus story and the significance of

unleavened bread. They can reflect on how these narratives apply to their own lives and the importance of living in obedience to God's commands.

5. *Worship Services:* Churches can hold special worship services throughout the week of the Feast of Unleavened Bread, focusing on themes of redemption, purity, and spiritual renewal. Worship can include singing hymns and songs that celebrate God's faithfulness and deliverance, as well as sermons or teachings that explore the biblical significance of the feast.

6. *Fellowship and Community:* Participants can gather with fellow believers for times of fellowship and community during the Feast of Unleavened Bread. This can involve sharing meals together, engaging in times of prayer and worship, and encouraging one another in their faith journeys. It's an opportunity to build deeper connections

with one another and to strengthen their commitment to following God.

7. *Acts of Service and Charity:* Believers can use the Feast of Unleavened Bread as a time to engage in acts of service and charity, reflecting God's heart for justice and compassion. This can involve volunteering in the community, serving those in need, or participating in outreach initiatives that demonstrate God's love in practical ways.

Overall, celebrating the Feast of Unleavened Bread is an opportunity for followers of Christ to deepen their relationship with God, grow in spiritual maturity, and renew their commitment to living lives of holiness and obedience. By engaging in practices that emphasize purity, reflection, worship, and service, believers can honor the significance of this feast and draw closer to God in their faith journey.

Feast of First Fruits

He Has Risen! The Feast of the Firstfruits represents the resurrection of our Lord and Savior Jesus Christ. Firstfruits is a significant holiday in Hebrew tradition and holds profound spiritual significance for all believers. This feast occurs during the Passover season and marks the offering of the first fruits of the barley harvest to God. It symbolizes gratitude for God's provision and acknowledges His sovereignty over the harvest.

In the Old Testament, the Feast of Firstfruits was observed by bringing a sheaf of the first ripe barley to the priest, who would wave it before the Lord as a symbol of dedication and gratitude. This offering represented the beginning of the harvest season and expressed trust in God's ongoing provision for His people.

In the New Testament, the Feast of Firstfruits holds special significance because it is the celebration of Jesus Christ's resurrection from the dead. The New Testament identifies Jesus as the "firstfruits" of those who have fallen asleep (1 Corinthians 15:20), signifying His victory over death and the promise of resurrection for all believers.

The connection between the Feast of Firstfruits and Jesus Christ's resurrection is deeply rooted in biblical typology. Just as the offering of the first fruits represented the beginning of the harvest season, so too does Jesus' resurrection mark the beginning of a new spiritual harvest—the resurrection of all believers to eternal life.

The Apostle Paul expounds upon this typology in his first letter to the Corinthians, where he writes, "But now is Christ risen from the dead, and become the firstfruits of them that slept. For since by man came death, by man came also the resurrection of the dead. For as in Adam all die, even so in Christ shall all be made alive."

In this passage, Paul emphasizes the significance of Jesus Christ's resurrection as the "firstfruits" of those who have fallen asleep, meaning those who have died in faith. He draws a parallel between

Adam, the first man, through whom death entered the world due to sin, and Jesus Christ, the second Adam, who brings resurrection and eternal life to all who believe in Him.

Paul's use of the term "firstfruits" underscores the idea that Jesus' resurrection inaugurates a new spiritual harvest, symbolizing the beginning of a broader resurrection of believers to eternal life. Just as the offering of first fruits in the Old Testament represented the dedication and gratitude for God's provision, so too does Jesus' resurrection signify God's redemptive plan for humanity and His victory over sin and death.

By highlighting the contrast between Adam, who brought sin and death into the world, and Jesus Christ, who brings righteousness and life, Paul emphasizes the transformative power of Christ's resurrection for all believers. Through faith in Jesus, believers are united with Him in His death and resurrection, sharing in the promise of eternal life and the hope of resurrection to come.

Overall, this passage from 1 Corinthians underscores the theological significance of Jesus Christ's resurrection as the firstfruits of a new spiritual harvest, marking the beginning of God's redemptive work in restoring humanity to Himself.

Therefore, the Feast of Firstfruits serves as a powerful reminder of God's faithfulness, His provision, and His redemptive plan for humanity. As believers commemorate this feast, they are invited to reflect on the significance of Jesus' resurrection, His victory over sin and death, and the hope of eternal life that He offers to all who believe.

The Resurrection:

The resurrection of Jesus Christ is the most pivotal event in New Testament theology, holding profound significance for believers and shaping the core doctrines of the faith. Its importance transcends historical significance, touching upon spiritual, theological, and existential dimensions that underpin the Christ led worldview and inform the lived experience of believers.

First and foremost, the resurrection of Jesus validates His claims to be the Son of God and the fulfillment of Old Testament prophecy. Throughout His ministry, Jesus asserted His divine identity and proclaimed Himself as the Messiah foretold by the prophets. His resurrection from the dead serves as the ultimate confirmation of this truth and His authority. As the Apostle Paul asserts in Romans 1:4, Jesus "was declared to be the Son of God with power, according to the spirit of holiness, by the resurrection from the dead." The resurrection affirms Jesus' divine nature, establishing Him as the central figure of human history and the source of salvation for all who believe in Him.

Moreover, the resurrection holds profound theological significance, particularly in relation to the doctrine of salvation. Through His death and resurrection, Jesus accomplished the atonement for humanity's sin, reconciling humanity with God and providing the means for forgiveness and redemption. As Paul declares in 1 Corinthians 15:17, "if Christ be not raised, your faith is vain; ye are yet in your sins." The resurrection demonstrates God's victory over sin and death, offering believers the assurance of forgiveness and eternal life through faith in Jesus Christ.

Furthermore, the resurrection serves as the prototype and guarantee of believers' own resurrection to eternal life. Just as Jesus was raised from the dead, so too will those who are united with Him through faith experience resurrection and transformation. The Apostle Paul affirms this hope in 1 Corinthians 15:20, declaring, "But now is Christ risen from the dead, and become the firstfruits of them that slept." The resurrection assures believers of their future resurrection and the fulfillment of God's promise of eternal life in His presence.

Existentially, the resurrection offers believers hope and assurance in the face of suffering, adversity, and death. It assures them that the power of death has been overcome and that ultimately, they will share in Christ's victory over the grave. As Paul writes in 1 Corinthians 15:54-55, "So when this corruptible shall have put on incorruption, and this mortal shall have put on immortality, then shall be brought to pass the saying that is written, Death is swallowed up in victory. O death, where is thy sting? O grave, where is thy victory?" The resurrection infuses life with meaning and purpose, providing comfort, strength, and assurance in times of trial and uncertainty.

The resurrection of Jesus Christ is of paramount importance to the faith of believers, serving as the linchpin of the belief system and the foundation of our hope. It validates Jesus' divine identity, confirms the truth claims of Christ's disciples, shapes core theological doctrines, and offers believers the assurance of forgiveness, salvation, and eternal life. The resurrection transforms lives, empowers faith, and illuminates the path to reconciliation with God, making it the most pivotal event in human history and the ultimate expression of God's love and grace toward humanity.

How to Celebrate:

For believers who wish to celebrate the Feast of Firstfruits, the focus is on adhering closely to biblical principles and practices. Here are some ways to celebrate the Feast of Firstfruits in a manner that honors biblical principles:

1. *Scripture Reading and Study*: Begin the celebration by reading and reflecting on biblical passages related to the Feast of Firstfruits and Jesus' resurrection. Key passages include 1 Corinthians 15, which discusses the significance of Christ as the firstfruits of the resurrection, and the Gospel accounts of Jesus' resurrection.

2. *Worship Service*: Attend or host a worship service that focuses on the resurrection of Jesus Christ. Worship should include singing hymns and songs that exalt Christ's victory over death and celebrate His resurrection. Sermons or teachings should center on the biblical significance of the Feast of Firstfruits and its fulfillment in Jesus' resurrection.

3. *Prayer and Thankfulness*: Set aside time for prayer and thanksgiving, expressing gratitude to God for the gift of salvation through Jesus Christ's resurrection. Offer prayers of praise, adoration, and thanksgiving for the hope and new life found in Christ.

4. *Holy Communion*: Participate in the sacrament of Holy Communion or the Lord's Supper as a symbolic remembrance of Jesus' sacrifice and resurrection. Focus on the spiritual significance of the bread and wine representing Christ's body and blood, which

were given for the forgiveness of sins and the promise of eternal life.

5. *Feasting and Fellowship*: Gather with fellow believers for a celebratory meal that emphasizes biblical principles of hospitality, generosity, and unity. Enjoy food and fellowship together, giving thanks for the abundance provided by God and the spiritual blessings found in Christ. Remember, this is still during the week of unleavened bread so do not have any leaven during this meal.

6. *Acts of Service and Compassion*: Take the opportunity to engage in acts of service and compassion as a reflection of Christ's love and compassion for others. Consider serving those in need, visiting the sick or elderly, or volunteering in the community as a tangible expression of Christ's resurrection power in action.

7. *Focus on Spiritual Renewal*: Use the Feast of Firstfruits as a time for personal and spiritual

renewal, committing to grow deeper in relationship with God and to live out the principles of the Christian faith in daily life. Consider practices such as fasting, prayer, and meditation on Scripture to draw closer to God and experience spiritual transformation.

By emphasizing biblical principles believers can celebrate the Feast of Firstfruits in a manner that honors God and focuses on the true spiritual significance of Jesus' resurrection.

Pentecost

The significance of Pentecost spans both the Old and New Testaments, representing a pivotal moment in the history of God's relationship with His people and the outpouring of His Spirit. In both contexts, Pentecost holds profound spiritual significance, marking moments of divine revelation, empowerment, and the inauguration of new covenants. Let's explore the significance of Pentecost in the Old Testament and New Testament, drawing from verses.

Pentecost in the Old Testament:

In the Old Testament, Pentecost is known as the Feast of Weeks or Shavuot, celebrated fifty days after the Passover. Its significance lies primarily in its agricultural context as a harvest festival, marking the end of the wheat harvest and the offering of firstfruits to God. However, Pentecost also carries theological and historical significance for the Israelites.

One key aspect of Pentecost in the Old Testament is its association with the giving of the Law at Mount Sinai. It was on Pentecost that God gave the Torah, or Law, to Moses, thereby establishing the covenant between God and Israel. This event is described in Exodus 19:1-6 and Exodus 20:1-21, where God descends upon Mount Sinai in fire and smoke, accompanied by thunder and lightning, and speaks the Ten Commandments to the people.

Exodus 19:1-6: "In the third month, when the children of Israel were gone forth out of the land of Egypt, the same day came they into the wilderness of Sinai. For they were departed from Rephidim, and were come to the desert of Sinai, and had pitched in the wilderness; and there Israel camped before the mount. And Moses went up unto God, and the Lord called unto him out of the mountain, saying, Thus shalt thou say to the house of Jacob, and tell the children of Israel; Ye have seen what I did unto the Egyptians, and how I bare you on eagles' wings, and brought you unto myself. Now therefore, if ye will obey my voice indeed, and keep my covenant, then ye shall be a peculiar treasure unto me above all people: for all the earth is mine: And ye shall be unto me a kingdom of priests, and an holy nation. These are the words which thou shalt speak unto the children of Israel."

Exodus 20:1-21: "And God spake all these words, saying, I am the Lord thy God, which have brought thee out of the land of Egypt, out of the house of bondage. Thou shalt have no other gods before me..."

This event marked the birth of Israel as a nation and established the covenant relationship between God and His chosen people. It laid the foundation for Israel's identity as a holy nation and set forth the moral and ethical standards by which they were to live.

Pentecost in the New Testament:

In the New Testament, Pentecost takes on a new and expanded significance with the coming of the

Holy Spirit. This is described in Acts 2:1-4, where the disciples are gathered together in Jerusalem during the Hebrew festival of Pentecost, and suddenly the Holy Spirit descends upon them in the form of tongues of fire, enabling them to speak in other languages.

Acts 2:1-4: "And when the day of Pentecost was fully come, they were all with one accord in one place. And suddenly there came a sound from heaven as of a rushing mighty wind, and it filled all the house where they were sitting. And there appeared unto them cloven tongues like as of fire, and it sat upon each of them. And they were all filled with the Holy Ghost, and began to speak with other tongues, as the Spirit gave them utterance."

This event marked the birth of the Church and the empowerment of believers for ministry. It fulfilled Jesus' promise to send the Holy Spirit as a helper and advocate (John 14:26) and inaugurated a new era of spiritual revelation and empowerment.

John 14:26: "But the Comforter, which is the Holy Ghost, whom the Father will send in my name, he shall teach you all things, and bring all things to your remembrance, whatsoever I have said unto you."

Pentecost in the New Testament is significant for several reasons:

1. *Empowerment for Witness:* The outpouring of the Holy Spirit at Pentecost empowered the disciples to boldly proclaim the gospel message to people of all nations. This is evidenced by Peter's sermon in Acts 2:14-41, where he declares the truth of Jesus' resurrection and calls for repentance and faith in Him.

2. *Inclusivity of the Gospel:* The miracle of speaking in tongues at Pentecost demonstrated the universality of the gospel message and its ability to transcend cultural and linguistic barriers. This foreshadowed the mission of the Church to proclaim the

gospel to all peoples, tongues, and nations (Matthew 28:19).

Matthew 28:19: "Go ye therefore, and teach all nations, baptizing them in the name of the Father, and of the Son, and of the Holy Ghost."

3. *Fulfillment of Prophecy:* Pentecost also fulfills the prophecy of Joel 2:28-32, where God promises to pour out His Spirit upon all flesh in the last days. Peter cites this prophecy in his sermon at Pentecost, affirming that its fulfillment has come with the outpouring of the Holy Spirit.

Joel 2:28-32: "And it shall come to pass afterward, that I will pour out my spirit upon all flesh; and your sons and your daughters shall prophesy, your old men shall dream dreams, your young men shall see visions: And also upon the servants and upon the handmaids in those days will I pour out my spirit."

Pentecost holds significant spiritual and theological implications in both the Old and New Testaments. In the Old Testament, it marks the giving of the Law at Mount Sinai and the establishment of the covenant between God and Israel. In the New Testament, Pentecost signifies the outpouring of the Holy Spirit and the birth of the Church, empowering believers for witness and ministry. Together, these events demonstrate God's faithfulness to His people and His ongoing work of redemption and renewal in the world.

How to Celebrate:

Celebrating Pentecost holds profound significance for believers, as it commemorates the outpouring of the Holy Spirit upon the early believers and the birth of the Church. This event, recorded in the book of Acts, marks a pivotal moment in the history of the church of Christ and carries timeless spiritual truths for believers today. Here's how believers can celebrate Pentecost in a meaningful and reflective manner:

1. *Prayer and Reflection*: Pentecost is a time for believers to engage in prayer and reflection, seeking a fresh outpouring of the Holy Spirit in their lives and communities. They can reflect on the significance of Pentecost as the fulfillment of Jesus' promise to send the Holy Spirit as a helper and advocate (John 14:26). Through prayer, believers can invite the Holy Spirit to work in their hearts and lives, empowering them for ministry and guiding them in the truth.

2. *Worship Services*: Churches can hold special worship services on Pentecost Sunday, focusing on themes of the Holy Spirit, empowerment for ministry, and the unity of the body of Christ. Worship can include singing hymns and songs that celebrate the work of the Holy Spirit, as well as prayers and readings from Scripture that highlight the

significance of Pentecost. Sermons or teachings can explore the biblical narrative of Pentecost and its implications for believers today, encouraging them to walk in the power and guidance of the Holy Spirit.

3. *Observance of Sacraments:* Pentecost is an opportune time for Christians to participate in the sacraments of baptism and communion. Baptism symbolizes the believer's identification with Christ's death, burial, and resurrection, while communion commemorates Jesus' sacrifice and the unity of the body of Christ. These sacraments serve as tangible expressions of faith and devotion, reaffirming believers' commitment to follow Christ and live in fellowship with one another.

4. *Community and Fellowship:* Pentecost provides an opportunity for believers to gather in fellowship and community, strengthening their bonds of unity and

mutual support. Believers can share meals, engage in times of prayer and worship, and participate in activities that promote spiritual growth and encouragement. Pentecost is a reminder of the diversity and unity of the body of Christ, as believers from different backgrounds come together in worship and fellowship.

5. *Mission and Outreach:* Pentecost is a call to mission and outreach, as believers are empowered by the Holy Spirit to proclaim the gospel and make disciples of all nations (Matthew 28:19-20). Christians can use Pentecost as an opportunity to engage in evangelism and outreach initiatives, sharing the love of Christ with those in their communities and beyond. This may involve acts of service, evangelistic events, or initiatives that address the spiritual and practical needs of others.

6. *Renewal and Revival:* Pentecost is a time for spiritual renewal and revival, both individually and corporately. Believers can use this season to examine their hearts and lives, seeking repentance and spiritual renewal through the work of the Holy Spirit. Pentecost reminds Christians of the transformative power of God's Spirit to bring about personal and communal revival, leading to greater intimacy with God and effectiveness in ministry.

Celebrating Pentecost is an opportunity for believers to remember and reflect on the outpouring of the Holy Spirit and its significance for their lives and communities. Through prayer, worship, fellowship, mission, and renewal, believers can honor the legacy of Pentecost and embrace the ongoing work of the Holy Spirit in their lives and in the world. Pentecost serves as a reminder of God's faithfulness, His empowering presence, and His call to mission and ministry until the return of Christ.

Blowing of Trumpets

The Blowing of Trumpets, also known as the Feast of Trumpets, is a significant festival in the Biblical calendar with rich symbolism and meaning both in the Old and New Testaments. This celebration marks the beginning of the seventh month of the Hebrew calendar. It holds spiritual significance that extends beyond its historical context. Let's explore the Blowing of Trumpets and its symbolism in biblical context.

The Blowing of Trumpets in the Old Testament:

In the Old Testament, the Blowing of Trumpets is described in Leviticus 23:23-25 as one of the appointed feasts of the Lord:

Leviticus 23:23-25: "And the Lord spake unto Moses, saying, Speak unto the children of Israel, saying, In the seventh month, in the first day of the month, shall ye have a sabbath, a memorial of blowing of trumpets, an holy convocation. Ye shall do no servile work therein: but ye shall offer an offering made by fire unto the Lord."

The blowing of trumpets during this festival served several purposes:

1. *Call to Assembly:* The blowing of trumpets served as a call to assembly, signaling the beginning of a sacred time of worship and reflection. It called the people of Israel to gather together for a holy convocation, where they would offer sacrifices and seek God's presence.

2. *Reminder of God's Sovereignty:* The sound of the trumpets reminded the Israelites of God's sovereignty and kingship over their lives. It symbolized the trumpet blast of God's voice, calling His people to attention and reminding them of His authority and rule.

3. *Preparation for the Day of Atonement:* The Blowing of Trumpets occurred on the first

day of the seventh month, which marked the beginning of a period of preparation leading up to the Day of Atonement (Yom Kippur). It served as a wake-up call for the people to prepare their hearts and lives for the solemnity and repentance of the Day of Atonement.

4. *Anticipation of the Messiah:* The Blowing of Trumpets is associated with the anticipation of the coming of the Messiah. The trumpet blasts are seen as a call for repentance and a reminder of God's promise to send a Redeemer to His people.

The Blowing of Trumpets in the New Testament:

In the New Testament, the Blowing of Trumpets takes on added significance in light of its fulfillment in Jesus Christ. While the New Testament does not explicitly mention the Blowing of Trumpets, its themes and symbolism find resonance in the teachings of Jesus and the apostles.

1. *Call to Repentance:* Jesus frequently called people to repentance and readiness for the kingdom of God, echoing the themes of preparation and anticipation associated with the Blowing of Trumpets. In Matthew 4:17, Jesus proclaims, "Repent: for the kingdom of heaven is at hand."

2. *Return of Christ:* The New Testament also speaks of the return of Christ with the sound of a trumpet, signaling the culmination of God's redemptive plan and the establishment of His kingdom. In 1 Thessalonians 4:16-17, Paul writes, "For the Lord himself shall descend from heaven with a shout, with the voice of the archangel, and with the trump of God: and the dead in Christ shall rise first: Then we which are alive and remain shall be caught up together with them in the clouds, to meet the Lord in the air: and so shall we ever be with the Lord."

3. *Day of Judgment:* The trumpet blasts associated with the Blowing of Trumpets also foreshadow the final judgment, when all people will be called to account before God. In Revelation 11:15-18, John describes the sounding of trumpets heralding the coming judgment and the establishment of God's eternal kingdom.

The Blowing of Trumpets holds significant symbolism and meaning in both the Old and New Testaments. It serves as a call to assembly, a reminder of God's sovereignty, and a preparation for repentance and the Day of Atonement. Its themes of repentance, anticipation of the Messiah, and the return of Christ find fulfillment in Jesus' teachings and the hope of His second coming. As believers, we can reflect on the symbolism of the Blowing of Trumpets and its relevance to our lives, remembering God's sovereignty, His call to repentance, and the anticipation of His kingdom.

How to Celebrate:

Believers can draw many spiritual insights from the Feast of Trumpets. The blowing of trumpets is associated with themes of repentance, preparation, and anticipation of Christ's return. Here's how believers can reflect on and apply these principles in their lives:

1. Reflection and Repentance: Use the Feast of Trumpets as a time for introspection and repentance. Reflect on areas of your life where you may need to turn back to God, seek forgiveness, and make changes in alignment with His will.

2. *Prayer and Intercession*: Spend time in prayer, individually and corporately, seeking God's guidance, wisdom, and presence. Pray for spiritual renewal, both in your own life and in the life of the Church. Intercede for the needs of others and for the fulfillment of God's purposes in the world.

3. *Study of Scripture:* Dive into the Word of God and study passages related to the significance of trumpets in biblical history and prophecy. Reflect on how these themes point to Christ and His ultimate victory and return.

4. *Worship and Thanksgiving:* Set aside time for worship and thanksgiving, praising God for His faithfulness, sovereignty, and provision. Use music, hymns, and songs of worship to express adoration and gratitude to God for His blessings and promises.

5. *Fellowship and Community:* Gather with fellow believers for times of fellowship and encouragement. Share meals together, engage in meaningful conversations, and pray for one another's spiritual growth and well-being. Blow the rams horn to commemorate the day.

6. *Anticipation of Christ's Return:* Use the Feast of Trumpets as an opportunity to reflect on

the anticipation of Christ's return. Meditate on passages of Scripture that speak of Christ's second coming and the establishment of His kingdom. Live in readiness and expectation of His coming, striving to be faithful and obedient servants until that day.

7. *Acts of Kindness and Compassion:* Demonstrate the love of Christ through acts of kindness and compassion toward others. Look for opportunities to serve and bless those in need, embodying the values of mercy, justice, and grace.

Believers can draw spiritual insights from trumpets symbolism and significance. This includes themes of repentance, preparation for Christ's return, and anticipation of God's faithfulness. By reflecting on these principles and applying them in their lives, believers can deepen their relationship with God and live in readiness for the coming of His kingdom.

Day of Atonement

The Day of Atonement, also known as Yom Kippur, is one of the most solemn and significant days in the Biblical calendar. It is a day set apart for fasting, repentance, and seeking forgiveness for sins, both individually and collectively. The Day of Atonement carries profound spiritual significance, pointing to the need for reconciliation with God and the ultimate atonement provided by Jesus Christ. Let's explore the Day of Atonement in the Bible.

The Day of Atonement in the Old Testament:

The institution of the Day of Atonement is described in Leviticus 16, where God gives instructions to Moses regarding the observance of this sacred day:

Leviticus 16:29-30: "And this shall be a statute for ever unto you: that in the seventh month, on the tenth day of the month, ye shall afflict your souls, and do no work at all, whether it be one of your own country, or a stranger that sojourneth among you: For on that day shall the priest make an atonement for you, to cleanse you, that ye may be clean from all your sins before the Lord."

On the Day of Atonement, the high priest would enter the Most Holy Place of the tabernacle or temple to make atonement for the sins of the people. This involved offering sacrifices for his own sins and for the sins of the people, as well as performing rituals with blood and incense to cleanse and purify the sanctuary and the people from sin.

Leviticus 16:34: "And this shall be an everlasting statute unto you, to make an atonement for the children of Israel for all their sins once a year. And he did as the Lord commanded Moses."

The Day of Atonement served as a solemn reminder of the seriousness of sin and the need for reconciliation with God. It emphasized the importance of repentance, humility, and dependence on God's mercy and forgiveness.

The Day of Atonement in the New Testament:

While the Day of Atonement is not explicitly mentioned in the New Testament, its themes of repentance, forgiveness, and reconciliation find fulfillment in the person and work of Jesus Christ.

Hebrews 9:11-12: "But Christ being come an high priest of good things to come, by a greater and more perfect tabernacle, not made with hands, that is to say, not of this building; Neither by the blood of goats and calves, but by his own blood he entered in once into the holy place, having obtained eternal redemption for us."

Jesus is described as the ultimate High Priest who offered Himself as the perfect and final sacrifice for sin. His death on the cross provided atonement for the sins of humanity, once and for all, fulfilling the need for sacrificial offerings and rituals.

Hebrews 10:19-22: "Having therefore, brethren, boldness to enter into the holiest by the blood of Jesus, By a new and living way, which he hath consecrated for us, through the veil, that is to say, his flesh; And having an high priest over the house of God; Let us draw near with a true heart in full assurance of faith, having our hearts sprinkled from an evil conscience, and our bodies washed with pure water."

Through faith in Jesus Christ, believers have access to God's presence and forgiveness. His atoning sacrifice opens the way for reconciliation with God, enabling believers to approach Him with confidence and assurance.

The Day of Atonement holds significant spiritual significance. It serves as a solemn day of repentance and reconciliation with God through prayer and fasting. Its themes find fulfillment in the person and work of Jesus Christ, who offered Himself as the perfect and final sacrifice for sin, providing atonement and reconciliation for all who believe. As believers, we can look to Jesus as our ultimate High Priest and Savior, who has made eternal redemption possible through His death and resurrection.

How to Celebrate:

The spiritual principles and themes of this solemn day hold profound significance for believers. While the ceremonial aspects of the Day of Atonement, such as sacrifices and rituals performed by the high priest in the Old Testament are no longer observed due to the fulfillment of these practices in Jesus Christ, there are still meaningful ways believers should honor the principles of repentance, forgiveness, and reconciliation embodied in this sacred day. Here's how believers can follow the essence of the Day of Atonement in their spiritual lives:

1. *Repentance and Reflection:* Like the Israelites on the Day of Atonement, believers can use this time to engage in deep introspection and reflection on their lives. They can

examine their hearts, confess sins, and seek God's forgiveness. This involves acknowledging areas of disobedience or brokenness and turning back to God with sincere repentance.

2. *Prayer and Fasting:* The Day of Atonement is characterized by fasting and prayer as a means of humbling oneself before God and seeking His mercy and forgiveness. Believers fast for a 24 hour period consuming no food or beverage. This can be modified for various physical ailments or such thinks as pregnancy. During this fasting period, read scripture and focus the heart and mind on God's presence and seek His guidance and forgiveness for yourself and others.

3. *Seeking Reconciliation:* The Day of Atonement emphasizes the importance of reconciliation with God and others. Believers can use this time to seek reconciliation in their relationships, extending forgiveness to

those who have wronged them and seeking forgiveness from those they have wronged. This reflects the principles of forgiveness and reconciliation taught by Jesus.

4. *Restoration and Renewal:* The Day of Atonement symbolizes a time of restoration and renewal, both individually and corporately. Believers can use this time to seek spiritual renewal and restoration in their relationship with God. This may involve recommitting themselves to spiritual disciplines, such as Bible study, worship, and fellowship, that deepen their intimacy with God and strengthen their faith.

5. *Living in Light of Christ's Atonement:* While the ceremonial aspects of the Day of Atonement are no longer observed under the New Covenant, believers should reflect on the ultimate atonement provided by Jesus Christ through His death and resurrection. His sacrifice on the cross

provided forgiveness for sin and reconciliation with God for all who believe. Believers can live in light of this truth, gratefully accepting God's forgiveness and extending His grace to others.

Believers keep the Day of Atonement by engaging in practices of repentance, prayer, fasting, seeking reconciliation, and living in light of Christ's atoning sacrifice. The principles embodied in the Day of Atonement serve as a powerful reminder of God's mercy, forgiveness, and desire for reconciliation with His people, which believers can embrace and embody in their daily lives.

Feast of Tabernacles

The Feast of Tabernacles, also known as Sukkot, is one of the major festivals celebrated in the Bible, commemorating the Israelites' journey through the wilderness and their dependence on God's provision and protection. It is a joyous occasion marked by the construction of temporary shelters, or sukkahs, and the gathering of families for meals and celebrations. The Feast of Tabernacles holds significant spiritual symbolism and relevance for believers, particularly in its connection to Jesus Christ.

The Feast of Tabernacles in the Old Testament:

In the Old Testament, the Feast of Tabernacles is described in Leviticus 23:33-43 as one of the appointed feasts of the Lord. During this seven-day festival, the Israelites were instructed to live in temporary shelters or booths as a reminder of their time in the wilderness and God's provision for them.

Leviticus 23:42-43: "Ye shall dwell in booths seven days; all that are Israelites born shall dwell in booths: That your generations may know that I made the children of Israel to dwell in booths, when I brought them out of the land of Egypt: I am the Lord your God."

The Feast of Tabernacles served as a time of rejoicing and thanksgiving for God's faithfulness and provision, as well as a time of reflection on His covenant relationship with His people.

The Feast of Tabernacles in the New Testament:

In the New Testament, the Feast of Tabernacles takes on added significance in light of its connection to Jesus Christ. It records significant events that took place during this festival and highlight its spiritual symbolism.

1. *Jesus' Teaching at the Feast of Tabernacles*: In John 7, Jesus attends the Feast of Tabernacles in Jerusalem and teaches in the temple. He declares Himself to be the source

of living water, inviting all who are thirsty to come to Him and drink. This declaration carries profound spiritual significance, as Jesus is revealing Himself as the fulfillment of the feast's symbolism.

John 7:37-38: "In the last day, that great day of the feast, Jesus stood and cried, saying, If any man thirst, let him come unto me, and drink. He that believeth on me, as the scripture hath said, out of his belly shall flow rivers of living water."

2. *The Transfiguration*: Some scholars suggest that the Transfiguration, recorded in Matthew 17, Mark 9, and Luke 9, may have taken place during the Feast of Tabernacles. This event, where Jesus is transfigured before Peter, James, and John and seen talking with Moses and Elijah, emphasizes Jesus' divine identity and the fulfillment of the Law and the Prophets in Him.

3. *Anticipation of the Messianic Age:* The Feast of Tabernacles is associated with the hope of

the coming Messianic age, when God's kingdom will be established on earth and His presence will dwell among His people. In Revelation 21:3, this hope is realized as John sees a vision of the new Jerusalem, where God dwells with His people and wipes away every tear from their eyes.

Revelation 21:3: "And I heard a great voice out of heaven saying, Behold, the tabernacle of God is with men, and he will dwell with them, and they shall be his people, and God himself shall be with them, and be their God."

The Feast of Tabernacles holds significant spiritual symbolism and relevance for believers, particularly in its connection to Jesus Christ. Through His teachings, actions, and fulfillment of Old Testament prophecies, Jesus reveals Himself as the source of living water, the fulfillment of the hope of the Messianic age, and the embodiment of God's presence with His people. We can reflect on the symbolism of the Feast of Tabernacles and its fulfillment in Jesus Christ, rejoicing in His provision, celebrating His presence, and eagerly anticipating the fulfillment of God's kingdom on earth.

How to Celebrate:

While the Feast of Tabernacles, or Sukkot, can celebrate it in various ways to honor its spiritual significance and symbolism. Here are some ways believers might choose to celebrate the Feast of Tabernacles:

1. *Camping*: Camping during the Feast of Tabernacles, or Sukkot, can be a meaningful and symbolic experience for believers seeking to connect with the festival's themes of temporary dwelling and dependence on God's provision. Setting up tents or temporary shelters amidst nature provides a tangible reminder of the Israelites' journey through the wilderness and their reliance on

God's guidance and protection. Just as the Israelites lived in booths during Sukkot to commemorate God's faithfulness in providing for them, modern-day believers can use camping as a time of reflection, prayer, and fellowship. It offers an opportunity to disconnect from the busyness of daily life, immerse oneself in God's creation, and deepen one's spiritual connection with Him. Camping during the Feast of Tabernacles allows believers to experience firsthand the joy of dwelling in God's presence and the blessings of His provision.

2. *Feasting and Fellowship*: Like in Hebrew tradition, believers may gather together with family and friends for festive meals and celebrations throughout the duration of the Feast of Tabernacles. Sharing meals, engaging in meaningful conversations, and spending time in fellowship can deepen relationships and foster a sense of

community among believers. Again, this meal is not meant to be gluttonous as is the custom of pagan feasts.

3. *Reading Scripture and Reflection:* During the Feast of Tabernacles, believers should read passages of Scripture related to the festival's themes of God's provision, protection, and presence. Reflecting on these biblical truths can deepen one's understanding of God's faithfulness and His ongoing work in the lives of His people.

4. *Prayer and Worship:* Believers may use the Feast of Tabernacles as an opportunity for prayer and worship, seeking God's presence and guidance in their lives. This may involve individual or corporate times of prayer, praise, and worship, as well as singing hymns and songs that celebrate God's provision and faithfulness.

5. *Acts of Generosity and Service:* The Feast of Tabernacles emphasizes thanksgiving and

generosity toward others. Believers can use this time to engage in acts of kindness and service, reaching out to those in need and sharing God's blessings with others. This can include volunteering at local charities, donating food or clothing to those less fortunate, or simply extending hospitality to others.

6. *Teaching and Learning:* Take the opportunity during the Feast of Tabernacles to learn more about the festival's significance and symbolism. This may involve studying Scripture, reading books or articles on the subject, or participating in teachings or discussions within their church community.

7. *Expressing Gratitude:* Throughout the Feast of Tabernacles, believers can cultivate an attitude of gratitude and thanksgiving toward God for His provision, protection, and presence in their lives. Expressing gratitude through prayer, praise, and acts of

worship can deepen one's relationship with God and foster a heart of thankfulness.

While the specific ways in which believers celebrate the Feast of Tabernacles may vary, the underlying principles of thanksgiving, remembrance, and celebration of God's faithfulness remain central. By engaging in these practices, believers can honor the spiritual significance of the Feast of Tabernacles and grow in their relationship with God and others.

Sabbath

The Sabbath holds a central and significant place in the Bible. In the creation narrative of Genesis, God establishes the Sabbath as a day of rest and sanctification, setting aside the seventh day as holy and modeling the importance of rest and worship. This foundational principle is reiterated throughout the Bible, where the Sabbath is commanded as a sacred day of rest and devotion to God. Exodus 20:8-11, part of the Ten Commandments, explicitly instructs, "Remember the Sabbath day, to keep it holy. Six days shalt thou labour, and do all thy work: But the seventh day is the Sabbath of the Lord thy God: in it thou shalt not do any work, thou, nor thy son, nor thy daughter, thy manservant, nor thy maidservant, nor thy cattle, nor thy stranger that is within thy gates: For in six days the Lord made heaven and earth, the sea, and all that in them is, and rested the seventh day: wherefore the Lord blessed the Sabbath day, and hallowed it."

Throughout the Bible, the observance of the Sabbath is consistently emphasized as a sign of the covenant between God and His people, symbolizing their dependence on Him as their Creator and Redeemer. Leviticus 23 further outlines the Sabbath's role in the Lord's festival calendar, highlighting its significance as a day of rest and worship alongside other sacred observances. Additionally, the prophets frequently admonish Israel to honor the Sabbath and refrain from profaning it with secular activities, emphasizing its spiritual and moral significance.

In the New Testament, while the observance of the Sabbath is not abolished, Jesus brings a new perspective and understanding to its significance. He reaffirms the Sabbath's importance as a day of rest and worship but challenges legalistic interpretations that prioritize outward observance over the spirit of the law. In Mark 2:27-28, Jesus declares, "The Sabbath was made for man, and not man for the Sabbath: Therefore the Son of man is Lord also of the Sabbath." Here, Jesus emphasizes the intended purpose of the Sabbath—to provide rest and refreshment for humanity, rather than being burdened by legalistic regulations.

Moreover, Jesus' ministry often included acts of healing and restoration on the Sabbath, demonstrating God's compassion and mercy. While these actions were controversial among some religious leaders, they served to highlight the true spirit of the Sabbath—to bring healing, wholeness, and liberation to those in need. As believers, the principles of rest, worship, and reflection remain foundational. The Sabbath serves as a time to pause from the busyness of life, to reconnect with God and others, and to experience spiritual renewal and restoration. Ultimately, the Sabbath continues to remind believers of God's sovereignty, provision, and invitation to enter into His rest—a foretaste of the eternal Sabbath rest promised in Christ.

Timing of the Sabbath:

The Sabbath is to be worshipped on the seventh day of the calendar week. In our calendar system, the Sabbath begins at sundown on Friday and extends until nightfall on Saturday. This timing is based on the lunar calendar used in ancient Israelite culture, where days were reckoned from evening to evening. This understanding is reflected in the creation narrative, where each day is described as beginning with the evening: "And the evening and the morning were the first day" (Genesis 1:5, KJV). Thus, the Sabbath begins with the onset of Friday evening and concludes with the arrival of Saturday evening.

The Sabbath from sundown Friday until sundown Saturday carries symbolic significance beyond its historical and chronological associations. It serves as a tangible reminder of God's rest after creation, His covenant relationship with His people, and the completion of Christ's redemptive work. Moreover, the Sabbath period encompasses both the end of the workweek and the beginning of the new week, symbolizing the transition from labor to rest and from darkness to light.

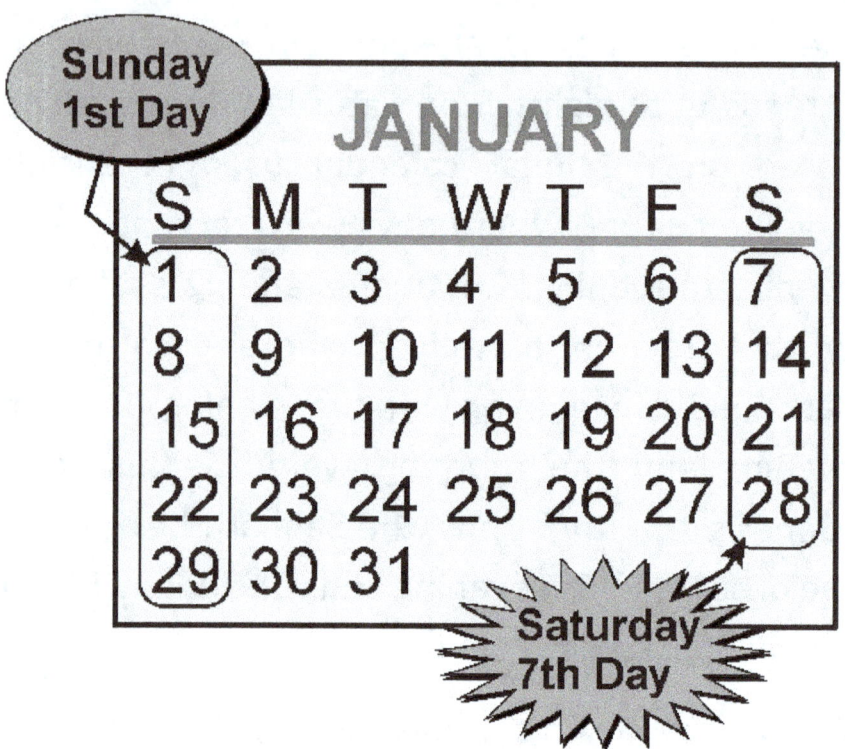

How to Keep the Sabbath:

Observing the Sabbath entails adhering to specific principles and guidelines outlined in the Scriptures. While interpretations and practices of

Sabbath observance may vary, there are common themes and principles that guide believers in honoring this sacred day. The Sabbath is intended as a time of rest, worship, and reflection, as well as a reminder of God's creative and redemptive work in the world.

In Exodus and Deuteronomy, God provides instructions for Sabbath observance, emphasizing the importance of ceasing from ordinary work and dedicating the day to rest and worship. Exodus 20:8-11, part of the Ten Commandments, commands: "Remember the Sabbath day, to keep it holy. Six days shalt thou labour, and do all thy work: But the seventh day is the Sabbath of the Lord thy God: in it thou shalt not do any work, thou, nor thy son, nor thy daughter, thy manservant, nor thy maidservant, nor thy cattle, nor thy stranger that is within thy gates: For in six days the Lord made heaven and earth, the sea, and all that in them is, and rested the seventh day: wherefore the Lord blessed the Sabbath day, and hallowed it." The Bible also states, "Six days shall work be done, but on the seventh day is a Sabbath of solemn rest, a holy convocation; ye shall do no manner of work; it is a Sabbath unto the Lord in all your dwellings" (Leviticus 23:3). This prohibition against work encompasses various forms of labor, including agricultural work, buying and selling, trade, and craftsmanship. The intention behind this restriction is to provide both humans and animals with a day of rest and rejuvenation, mirroring God's rest after the work of creation (Genesis 2:2-3).

Furthermore, the biblical text highlights the importance of refraining from activities that involve preparation or acquisition, such as cooking, baking, and gathering food. In Exodus 16:23-30, God provides manna to the Israelites in the wilderness and instructs them to gather enough food for two days on the sixth day of the week, as no manna would be provided on the Sabbath. This serves as a demonstration of God's provision and a reminder to trust in His faithfulness.

In addition to abstaining from work and preparation, the biblical text emphasizes the importance of dedicating the Sabbath day to worship and spiritual reflection. Isaiah 58:13-14 exhorts believers to "call the Sabbath a delight, the holy of Yahweh, honorable; and shalt honor it, not doing thine own ways, nor finding thine own pleasure, nor speaking thine own words: then shalt thou delight thyself in Yahweh; and I will make thee to ride upon the high places of the earth."

While the biblical text provides general principles for Sabbath observance, the interpretation and application of these principles may vary among different traditions and communities. Nevertheless, the overarching emphasis on rest, worship, and sanctification remains central to Sabbath observance, serving as a timeless reminder of God's sovereignty, provision, and invitation to enter into His rest. Through Sabbath observance, believers have the opportunity to experience spiritual renewal, deepen their relationship with God, and honor the timeless traditions of their faith.

New Moons

In the Bible, the concept of new moons holds significance within the framework of ceremonial observance and the worship calendar. New moons, or the beginning of each lunar month, were marked as special occasions for sacred observance, sacrifices, and gatherings. The importance of new moons is reflected in various passages throughout the Bible, where they are mentioned alongside other sacred festivals and observances.

One of the primary references to new moons is found in Numbers 28:11-15, where God commands the Israelites to offer sacrifices on the first day of each month in addition to their regular offerings. These sacrifices were to be presented as a pleasing aroma to the Lord and served as a symbol of the Israelites' ongoing commitment to worship and obedience.

Another significant mention of new moons is found in Isaiah 1:13-14, where the prophet Isaiah rebukes the Israelites for their hypocritical observance of religious rituals, including new moon celebrations. Despite their outward adherence to religious practices, their hearts were far from God, and their offerings were unacceptable in His sight. Isaiah emphasizes the importance of genuine repentance and obedience over empty ritualism.

In addition to these explicit references, new moons are also mentioned in the context of various historical accounts and poetic passages throughout the Scriptures. For example, the Psalms often make reference to new moons as occasions for praise and worship (Psalm 81:3; 104:19). Similarly, the books of Chronicles and Kings record the observance of new moons alongside other religious festivals and events.

In the New Testament, the concept of new beginnings and the lunar calendar's rhythm remains a part of the biblical narrative. In the book of Colossians, the apostle Paul warns against being judged by others regarding the observance of new moons and other religious rituals, emphasizing instead the centrality of Christ and His redemptive work (Colossians 2:16-17). Paul's words remind believers that true worship is found in Christ alone, rather than in outward observance of rituals.

The New Moons serve as a reminder of God's sovereignty and faithfulness in sustaining His creation. The lunar cycle, with its phases of waxing and waning, reflects the cyclical nature of time and the ongoing work of God in the world. Celebrating the New Moons can foster a sense of awe and wonder at God's handiwork in the heavens and inspire believers to praise Him as the Creator and Sustainer of all things.

Moreover, the New Moons can serve as a time of spiritual renewal and reflection for believers. In a world filled with busyness and distractions, setting aside time to observe the New Moons allows believers to pause, reflect, and realign their hearts with God's purposes. It provides an opportunity for introspection, prayer, and seeking God's guidance for the month ahead, as well as for expressing gratitude for His blessings and provision.

Additionally, celebrating the New Moons can foster a sense of community and fellowship among believers. Gathering together with fellow believers to observe the New Moons provides an opportunity for mutual encouragement, support, and edification. It allows believers to share in times of worship, prayer, and reflection, deepening their bonds of friendship and unity in Christ.

How to Celebrate:

The observance of New Moons often included gatherings for worship and celebration. Psalm 81:3 describes the blowing of trumpets and the singing of praises on the New Moon, while Isaiah 66:23 speaks of New Moons as occasions for worship and homage to God. Believers can engage in various practices to honor this occasion and deepen their spiritual connection with God. Here are some activities that can be done on New Moons:

1. *Worship and Prayer:* Set aside time for personal or communal worship, prayer, and meditation. Reflect on God's goodness, offer thanksgiving for His blessings, and seek His guidance for the month ahead.

2. *Scripture Reading:* Spend time reading and studying the Bible, focusing on passages that speak to themes of renewal, new beginnings, and God's faithfulness.

3. *Fellowship:* Gather with fellow believers for fellowship, encouragement, and mutual edification. Share testimonies, pray for one another, and uplift each other in faith.

4. *Reflection and Journaling:* Take time to reflect on the previous month and set goals

or intentions for the month ahead. Journal your thoughts, prayers, and reflections on God's faithfulness in your life.

5. *Nature Walk:* Connect with God's creation by spending time outdoors. Take a nature walk, hike, or picnic, and marvel at the beauty and intricacy of God's handiwork.

6. *Creative Expression:* Engage in creative activities such as writing, painting, or music that allow you to express your gratitude and worship to God.

7. *Acts of Kindness:* Look for opportunities to show love and kindness to others, whether through acts of service, generosity, or hospitality.

8. *Rest and Relaxation:* Embrace the spirit of rest and rejuvenation by taking time to rest and relax. Practice self-care activities that nurture your physical, emotional, and spiritual well-being.

9. *Setting Intentions:* Set intentions or goals for personal growth, spiritual development, or service to others. Commit these intentions to God in prayer and seek His guidance in fulfilling them.

Purim

The festival of Purim, mentioned in the Book of Esther, commemorates the deliverance of the Israelite people from a plot to exterminate them in ancient Persia. The festival is celebrated with joyous festivities, reading of the Book of Esther (Megillah), giving to the poor, feasting, and exchanging gifts.

The story of Purim, as recounted in the Book of Esther, revolves around Queen Esther, who, with the help of her cousin Mordecai, exposes a plot by the villainous Haman to annihilate the Israelite population of Persia. Through Esther's courage and Mordecai's wisdom, the Israelite people are spared from destruction, and Haman and his allies are defeated. The miraculous deliverance of the Israelite people is attributed to God's providence and intervention, even though His name is not explicitly mentioned in the Book of Esther.

Purim is celebrated annually on the 14th day of the twelfth Hebrew month, which typically falls in late

February or early March on the Gregorian calendar. The festivities begin on the evening of the 13th day with the reading of the Book of Esther. During the reading, whenever Haman's name is mentioned, it is customary for the congregation to drown out his name with noise-makers or booing, symbolizing the defeat of evil.

On the day of Purim itself, the celebrations continue with festive meals, known as Seudat Purim, where family and friends come together to feast and rejoice. It is also a time for giving to the poor and providing assistance to those in need, in keeping with the biblical injunction to "send portions to those for whom nothing is prepared" (Esther 9:22).

Another significant aspect of Purim is the custom of exchanging gifts with family, friends, and neighbors. This practice fosters unity and goodwill within the community and serves as a reminder of the importance of generosity and kindness.

Overall, the festival of Purim is a joyous celebration of deliverance and salvation, reminding believers of God's faithfulness and protection even in the most challenging circumstances. Through its customs and traditions, Purim encourages unity, generosity, and gratitude, while also providing an opportunity for reflection on the enduring lessons of the biblical narrative.

Hanukkah

Hanukkah, also known as the Festival of Lights, is a significant Israelite holiday commemorating the rededication of the Second Temple in Jerusalem after its desecration by the forces of Antiochus IV Epiphanes in the 2nd century BCE.

The story of Hanukkah is rooted in the events of the Maccabean Revolt, during which a small band of Israelite warriors, led by Judah Maccabee and his brothers, rebelled against the oppressive rule of the Seleucid Empire. After reclaiming the Temple from the Greek forces, the Maccabees found it desecrated and in need of purification.

The central ritual of Hanukkah is the lighting of the Hanukkah menorah, a seven-branched candelabrum. The menorah is placed in a prominent location, such as a window or doorway, to publicize the miracle of Hanukkah and symbolize the victory of light over darkness. In addition to candle lighting, families gather together to enjoy festive foods, exchange gifts, and play traditional games.

The New Testament mentions Jesus attending the Feast of Dedication (John 10:22-23), which is understood to refer to Hanukkah. "And it was at Jerusalem the feast of the dedication, and it was winter. And Jesus walked in the temple in Solomon's porch." This passage holds significant meaning both historically and symbolically within the context of Jesus' ministry and the Lord's ceremonial calendar. By attending this festival, Jesus acknowledges and participates in the ceremonial observance of His Hebrew community.

Jesus' presence at the Temple during Hanukkah holds symbolic significance within the narrative of John's Gospel. The themes of light and dedication associated with Hanukkah parallel Jesus' own identity and mission as the Light of the World and the fulfillment of God's redemptive plan. By walking in the Temple during Hanukkah, Jesus reaffirms His role as the long-awaited Messiah who brings spiritual illumination and renewal to God's people. The setting of this passage in the winter during Hanukkah also carries symbolic significance. Winter is often associated with darkness and coldness, yet Jesus, the Light of the World, enters the Temple to bring warmth, light, and spiritual renewal. This foreshadows Jesus' ultimate mission to bring salvation and eternal life to humanity through His sacrificial death and resurrection.

Hanukkah carries profound themes of faith, freedom, and perseverance, resonating with believers of all backgrounds. It serves as a reminder of God's faithfulness, His miraculous intervention on behalf of His people, and the enduring legacy of those who stood against oppression in defense of religious freedom. Through its rituals, symbols, and traditions, Hanukkah continues to inspire believers worldwide to celebrate their heritage, affirm their identity, and reaffirm their commitment to God and His promises.

Pagan Rituals

Believers should exercise caution and discernment when considering participation in pagan holidays due to the biblical principles of spiritual purity and devotion to God. While the Bible does not explicitly address every cultural practice or holiday observance, it consistently warns against adopting the religious rituals and customs of pagan nations. Scripture emphasizes the importance of maintaining distinctiveness in worship and avoiding entanglements with practices that compromise faithfulness to God. By refraining from involvement in activities associated with pagan rituals and idolatry, believers uphold the biblical mandate to worship God alone and to live lives that reflect His holiness and truth.

One key biblical principle that pertains to this question is found in the Old Testament, particularly in passages such as Deuteronomy 12:30-31, where God commands His people to avoid adopting the religious practices of the surrounding nations: "Take heed to thyself that thou be not snared by following them, after that they be destroyed from before thee; and that thou inquire not after their gods, saying, How did these nations serve their gods? even so will I do likewise. Thou shalt not do so unto the Lord thy God: for every abomination to the Lord, which he hateth, have they done unto their gods; for even their sons and their daughters they have burnt in the fire to their gods."

This passage underscores the importance of maintaining distinctiveness in worship and refraining from adopting the customs and rituals associated with pagan religions. God warns His people against following the practices of the nations around them, emphasizing that such actions are abominable in His sight.

Furthermore, the New Testament contains passages that urge believers to be cautious about participating in activities that may compromise their faith or lead them away from devotion to

God. In 2 Corinthians 6:14-18, the apostle Paul admonishes believers to avoid being unequally yoked with unbelievers and to separate themselves from anything that is contrary to God's will: "Be ye not unequally yoked together with unbelievers: for what fellowship hath righteousness with unrighteousness? and what communion hath light with darkness? And what concord hath Christ with Belial? or what part hath he that believeth with an infidel? And what agreement hath the temple of God with idols? for ye are the temple of the living God; as God hath said, I will dwell in them, and walk in them; and I will be their God, and they shall be my people. Wherefore come out from among them, and be ye separate, saith the Lord, and touch not the unclean thing; and I will receive you, And will be a Father unto you, and ye shall be my sons and daughters, saith the Lord Almighty."

These verses emphasize the need for believers to maintain spiritual purity and to avoid entanglements with practices that compromise their commitment to Christ. While the specific context of these passages may not directly address holiday observance, the underlying principle of spiritual separation from idolatry and ungodliness is applicable to the question of participation in holidays with pagan origins.

Additionally, in 1 Corinthians 10:20-22, Paul warns against partaking in the rituals associated with pagan worship, emphasizing that believers cannot simultaneously participate in the table of the Lord and the table of demons: "But I say, that the things which the Gentiles sacrifice, they sacrifice to devils, and not to God: and I would not that ye should have fellowship with devils. Ye cannot drink the cup of the Lord, and the cup of devils: ye cannot be partakers of the Lord's table, and of the table of devils. Do we provoke the Lord to jealousy? are we stronger than he?"

These verses underscore the incompatibility of worshipping the Lord with practices rooted in pagan idolatry. Believers are called to be vigilant in guarding their hearts and minds against any form of compromise that may dilute their allegiance to Christ and His teachings.

While the Bible does not explicitly address every specific holiday or cultural practice, its overarching principles provide guidance for believers seeking to navigate the complexities of modern life in a manner that honors God. By applying the biblical principles of spiritual purity, discernment, and separation from idolatry, believers can prayerfully evaluate their participation in holiday observances with pagan origins and strive to maintain fidelity to their faith in Jesus Christ.

Easter

The holiday of Easter, widely celebrated by Christians around the world, has roots that trace back to pre-Christian pagan traditions. The name "Easter" itself is derived from Eostre, a Germanic goddess associated with fertility and the dawn. The timing of Easter, which falls near the vernal equinox, also aligns with ancient spring fertility festivals that celebrated renewal and rebirth. Many customs and symbols associated with Easter, such as eggs, rabbits, and spring flowers, have pagan origins and were incorporated into Christian Easter celebrations over time.

Despite its widespread observance within the Christian community, the pagan origins and customs of Easter detract from its significance as a biblical holiday. Instead, The feasts of Passover, the Feast of Unleavened Bread, and the Feast of Firstfruits are the appropriate occasions for commemorating the crucifixion and resurrection of Jesus Christ. While historical records detailing the specific practices of Eostre worship are scarce, scholars have drawn connections between Eostre and the observance of spring fertility festivals that were common among ancient Germanic and Celtic peoples.

One aspect of Eostre's worship likely involved the celebration of the vernal equinox, a significant astronomical event marking the beginning of spring. This time of year was associated with the renewal of life, the awakening of nature from winter dormancy, and the promise of fertility and abundance in the coming growing season. Eostre's festival, held around the vernal equinox, would have featured rituals and ceremonies honoring her as a goddess of fertility and renewal.

One prominent custom associated with Eostre worship is the decoration of eggs, which symbolize fertility, new life, and the potential for growth. Eggs were often dyed in vibrant colors and decorated with intricate designs, then exchanged as gifts or offered as offerings to Eostre. The egg became a powerful symbol of the rebirth and regeneration associated with the goddess and the spring season.

Another common feature of Eostre celebrations may have been the use of hares or rabbits as symbols of fertility and abundance. These animals, known for their prolific breeding habits, were associated with Eostre as symbols of her fertility aspect. The hare or rabbit motif likely appeared in various forms of artwork, decorations, and rituals during Eostre festivities.

In addition to these customs, Eostre worship may have included rituals, prayers, and offerings to honor the goddess and seek her blessings for a fruitful and bountiful year ahead. These practices would have varied among different Germanic and Celtic communities, each adapting Eostre's worship to their own cultural traditions and beliefs.

Christmas

The holiday of Christmas, widely celebrated by Christians around the world, has origins that intertwine with pre-Christian pagan customs and traditions. While the Bible does not provide explicit instructions for celebrating the birth of Jesus Christ, various elements of modern Christmas observance have roots in ancient pagan practices. One such example is the tradition of decorating evergreen trees, a custom with ties to pagan winter solstice festivals that celebrated the renewal of life and the return of light.

In the book of Jeremiah, there is a passage that connects to the modern practice of decorating

Christmas trees. Jeremiah 10:3-4 states: "For the customs of the people are vain: for one cutteth a tree out of the forest, the work of the hands of the workman, with the axe. They deck it with silver and with gold; they fasten it with nails and with hammers, that it move not." While the context of this passage likely refers to the creation of idols, it is also a condemnation of the pagan practice of decorating trees for religious purposes.

Another aspect of Christmas with pagan origins is the timing of the holiday. December 25th was chosen by early Christian leaders to coincide with the winter solstice, an important date in many pre-Christian cultures. The winter solstice marked the shortest day and longest night of the year, symbolizing the rebirth of the sun and the gradual return of light and warmth. By aligning Christmas with the winter solstice, Christian leaders sought to co-opt existing pagan celebrations and provide a Christian alternative.

Additionally, the exchange of gifts during Christmas has parallels in ancient Roman festivals such as Saturnalia and the Roman New Year, during which gifts were exchanged as symbols of goodwill and friendship. Over time, the tradition of gift-giving became a central aspect of Christmas observance.

The Bible does not explicitly command the celebration of Jesus' birth or provide instructions for observing it. In fact, the Bible does not mention the celebration of birthdays in a positive light at all. There are only two mentions of birthdays in the Bible, both of which are associated with pagan rulers and events. In Genesis 40, Pharaoh's birthday is mentioned in the context of Joseph interpreting dreams, and in Matthew 14, Herod's birthday is linked to the execution of John the Baptist.

While Christmas is widely celebrated by Christians as a time to commemorate the birth of Jesus Christ, its origins and customs are deeply intertwined with pre-Christian pagan traditions. The decoration of evergreen trees, the timing of the holiday, and the exchange of gifts all have roots in ancient pagan practices. Furthermore, the Bible does not provide explicit instructions for celebrating Christmas, and the celebration of birthdays is not portrayed positively in Scripture. As such, believers should approach the observance of Christmas with discernment and avoid the adoption of pagan customs that detract from the true way to follow Christ.

Halloween

The holiday of Halloween, observed on October 31st, has origins that can be traced back to ancient Celtic pagan traditions, particularly the festival of Samhain. Samhain marked the end of the harvest season and the beginning of winter, a time when the boundary between the living and the dead was believed to be at its thinnest. During Samhain, the Celts believed that spirits and fairies could roam freely on earth, and rituals were performed to ward off malevolent entities and honor deceased ancestors.

One prominent custom associated with Samhain was the lighting of bonfires, which served both practical and symbolic purposes. Bonfires were believed to provide protection against evil spirits and were used to purify and cleanse the land for the coming winter. Additionally, the Celts would often wear costumes and masks during Samhain celebrations to disguise themselves from wandering spirits and to mimic the supernatural beings they believed roamed the earth.

Over time, as Christianity spread throughout Europe, pagan traditions like Samhain were gradually assimilated into Christian observances. In the 8th century, Pope Gregory III designated November 1st as All Saints' Day, a Christian holiday to honor saints and martyrs. The evening before All Saints' Day came to be known as All Hallows' Eve, which later evolved into Halloween.

While Halloween has become a secular holiday associated with costumes, candy, and spooky decorations, its pagan origins raise concerns about its compatibility with the faith and values of believers. Participating in Halloween celebrations, with their associations with death, the occult, and supernatural beings, conflicts with biblical principles of holiness and purity.

The Bible repeatedly warns against involvement in practices associated with witchcraft, sorcery, and the occult. In Deuteronomy 18:9-12, God commands His people to avoid divination, sorcery, and communication with spirits: "When thou art come into the land which the Lord thy God giveth thee, thou shalt not learn to do after the abominations of those nations. There shall not be found among you any one that maketh his son or his daughter to pass through the fire, or that useth divination, or an observer of times, or an enchanter, or a witch, Or a charmer, or a consulter with familiar spirits, or a wizard, or a necromancer. For all that do these things are an abomination unto the Lord: and because of these abominations the Lord thy God doth drive them out from before thee."

Furthermore, the apostle Paul admonishes believers to "abstain from all appearance of evil" (1 Thessalonians 5:22) and to "have no fellowship with the unfruitful works of darkness, but rather reprove them" (Ephesians 5:11). These passages underscore the importance of maintaining spiritual purity and avoiding participation in activities that promote darkness or compromise one's witness for Christ.

Thanksgiving

The true origins of Thanksgiving in the United States are deeply intertwined with a complex history of colonization, displacement, and violence against indigenous peoples. While the holiday is often associated with a narrative of Pilgrims and Native Americans coming together in peace and gratitude, this depiction overlooks the darker realities of conquest and exploitation that characterized the relationships between European settlers and indigenous communities.

The traditional story of the first Thanksgiving in 1621, which portrays Pilgrims and Wampanoag Indians sharing a harmonious meal to celebrate the harvest, is a sanitized version of history that obscures the deeper injustices of colonization. In reality, European settlement in North America brought about profound changes for indigenous peoples, including land dispossession, cultural erasure, and violence.

The arrival of European settlers, including the Pilgrims aboard the Mayflower, marked the beginning of a process of colonization that resulted in the displacement and marginalization of indigenous peoples. European colonists seized land from indigenous communities, forcibly removed them from their ancestral territories, and established settlements that disrupted traditional ways of life.

Moreover, the relationship between European settlers and indigenous peoples was often fraught with conflict and violence. Throughout the colonial period, there were numerous instances of warfare, massacres, and atrocities perpetrated against indigenous communities by European settlers and colonial authorities. These acts of violence, along with the spread of infectious diseases brought by Europeans, had devastating consequences for indigenous populations, leading to widespread death and suffering.

In the context of this history of colonization and violence, the notion of Thanksgiving as a peaceful gathering between Pilgrims and Native Americans takes on a more complex and troubling meaning. While it is true that indigenous peoples may have extended acts of kindness and hospitality towards European settlers in some instances, these gestures were often met with betrayal, exploitation, and ultimately, the erosion of indigenous sovereignty and autonomy.

Furthermore, the image of the turkey as the centerpiece of the Thanksgiving meal carries additional layers of symbolism when viewed through the lens of indigenous history. The turkey was indeed a sacred bird for many indigenous peoples, revered for its role in sustaining communities through hunting and gathering. However, the appropriation of the turkey as a symbol of Thanksgiving overlooks the deeper cultural significance it held for indigenous cultures and reinforces narratives of conquest and domination.

New Year's Eve

The celebration of New Year's Eve, observed on December 31st, has origins that can be traced back to ancient pagan customs and traditions. While the specific origins of New Year's Eve are somewhat obscure, the holiday's timing and associated rituals have connections to ancient winter solstice festivals and agricultural cycles. In the Biblical calendar, the New Year begins in the spring, a time of new life and growth.

One aspect of New Year's Eve with potential pagan origins is its timing, which falls close to the winter solstice, an astronomical event marking the shortest day and longest night of the year. In many ancient cultures, the winter solstice held great significance as a time of transition and renewal, symbolizing the return of light and the promise of new beginnings. Festivals and celebrations held around the winter solstice often involved rituals to ward off evil spirits, encourage the return of the sun, and ensure a prosperous year ahead.

In ancient Rome, the festival of Saturnalia, held in honor of the god Saturn, coincided with the winter solstice and was marked by feasting, merrymaking, and the exchange of gifts. Saturnalia was a time of revelry and excess, during which social norms were temporarily overturned, and masters and slaves would switch roles. Similarly, the Roman New Year, which originally fell on March 1st but was later moved to January 1st, was celebrated with ceremonies and rituals to invoke good fortune for the coming year.

In addition to the Roman festivals, other ancient cultures around the world observed similar customs and rituals to mark the transition from the old year to the new. In ancient Egypt, for example, the festival of Wepet Renpet celebrated the annual flooding of the Nile River, which brought fertility and abundance to the land. In Mesopotamia, the Babylonians held a festival called Akitu to honor the god Marduk and ensure a successful harvest in the coming year.

Today, New Year's Eve is celebrated in various ways around the world, with traditions ranging from fireworks and countdowns to midnight to feasting, parties, and cultural rituals. While the specific customs and practices associated with New Year's Eve may vary from one culture to another, the holiday continues to evoke themes of its ancient pagan origins.

New Year's Eve is often a time when sinful practices abound. In the midst of festivities and revelry, it is not uncommon for individuals to engage in excessive drinking, drug use, and reckless behavior. The party atmosphere of New Year's Eve can sometimes lead to a disregard for moral boundaries, with some people indulging in promiscuity, immorality, and other harmful activities. Moreover, the focus on hedonistic pleasure and self-indulgence can overshadow the true significance of the holiday, leading to a loss of perspective and spiritual neglect. As Believers, it is important to approach New Year's Eve with discernment and to resist the temptations of sinful behavior, instead choosing to honor God in our actions and attitudes.

Valentine's Day

The holiday of Valentine's Day, celebrated on February 14th, has origins that date back to ancient Roman pagan customs. While the precise historical origins of Valentine's Day are somewhat murky, it is widely believed to have been influenced by the ancient Roman festival of Lupercalia, which was held in mid-February to honor the god Lupercus, the god of fertility and agriculture.

During Lupercalia, young men would strip naked and run through the streets, striking women with strips of goat hide called "februa" in an effort to increase fertility. It was believed that being touched by the februa would make women more fertile and increase their chances of conception. This pagan festival also involved matchmaking rituals and celebrations of love and fertility.

Over time, the Christian church sought to Christianize pagan festivals like Lupercalia by replacing them with Christian feast days. In the 5th century, Pope Gelasius I declared February 14th as St. Valentine's Day, in honor of the martyrs Valentine of Rome and Valentine of Terni. However, the holiday retained some of its pagan customs and associations with love and fertility.

In medieval Europe, Valentine's Day became associated with romantic love and courtship, thanks in part to the influence of Chaucer and his poem "Parlement of Foules," which described February 14th as the day when birds chose their mates. By the 18th century, exchanging handwritten notes, flowers, and small tokens of affection became popular customs associated with Valentine's Day.

About the Author

Karajah Yashar graduated from Rutgers University, where he earned his degree in Anthropology. Karajah has worked professionally for both Rutgers and the University of Central Florida. Driven by a deep-seated passion for biblical literature and a desire to make scholarly works more accessible, Karajah founded Blackstone Publishing in Orlando, Florida.

Karajah's vision for Blackstone Publishing extends beyond mere publication; he seeks to foster a community of scholars and seekers who are dedicated to exploring the depths of biblical wisdom and understanding. Through his leadership, Blackstone Publishing continues to be a catalyst for intellectual growth and spiritual enlightenment, leaving an indelible mark on the world of biblical scholarship.